READY TO MAKE
MUSIC

IS THE
GUITAR
FOR YOU?

ELAINE LANDAU

Lerner Publications Company · Minneapolis

Lerner Publications Company
A division of Lerner Publishing Group, Inc.
 241 First Avenue North
      Minneapolis, MN 55401 U.S.A.

         Website address: www.lernerbooks.com

            Library of Congress Cataloging-in-Publication Data

            Landau, Elaine.
               Is the guitar for you? / by Elaine Landau.
                 p.   cm. — (Ready to make music)
               Includes bibliographical references and index.
               ISBN 978-0-7613-5424-6 (lib. bdg. : alk. paper)
               1. Guitar—Juvenile literature. I. Title.
            ML1015.G9L36 2011
               787.87′19—dc22   2009048750

            Manufactured in the United States of America
            1 – DP – 7/15/10

CONTENTS

CHAPTER ONE

IN THE GROOVE
WITH YOUR GUITAR

Picture this:

You're a guitarist in a rock band. You're not just any guitarist, though. Your guitar playing is your claim to fame. People call you a guitar hero.

Tonight's the first stop on your band's world tour. You're playing in a stadium packed with fans. You step onstage with your favorite guitar. It's bright red with shiny gold lightning bolts. The crowd goes wild. Once again, you live up to your reputation and, as always, rock the house!

Switch to this scene: You're a respected classical guitarist. You've been called the grand master of the guitar. People pay high prices for tickets to your performances. They know it's worth it to hear a world-class guitarist.

A Palestinian girl plays classical guitar in a competition in 2008.

You're on a fifty-city concert tour. You're performing for a full house. As you begin to play, the room goes silent. You can hear a pin drop. But when you finish, thunderous applause begins. People will be talking about your performance for months. You've done it again.

Can you see yourself in either of these scenes? Well, the guitar is extremely versatile. It's used to play many types of music. If you master it, either scene just might be possible.

Do you dream of mastering the guitar? That can be a terrific goal. There are lots of good reasons to study guitar. Here are just a few.

A POPULAR INSTRUMENT

If you want to play an instrument, the guitar may be the hippest one around. Need proof? Answer this: who's the coolest musician in a rock band? Was your answer the lead guitarist? If it was, you aced this quick quiz! The lead guitarist is often the fans' favorite.

ALL IN THE FAMILY

You come from a family. You may look or sound a lot like your family members. Do you have your dad's smile? Your mom's eyes? Or maybe you share your uncle Joe's wicked sense of humor.

Instruments are grouped in families too. The guitar is in the string family. The instruments in this family have some things in common. They all make sounds through the movement of their strings.

Many different instruments belong to the string family. They come in lots of shapes and sizes. Each one has its own special sound. Other string instruments include the violin, the cello, the banjo, and the double bass.

The violin (left) and the viola (right) are two other string instruments.

THE PRICE IS RIGHT

Some instruments are very pricey. It's hard to find a saxophone in good condition that doesn't cost a lot. This isn't so with a guitar. Guitars vary greatly in price. But you can always find a low-cost one to learn on.

Carlos Santana plays guitar at a jazz festival in Switzerland in 2004.

A GREAT SIZE

The guitar is small enough to carry around with you. That comes in handy. You can take it with you to a party or a friend's house. Don't try that with a piano.

YOU GOTTA LOVE IT

Don't forget the most important reason to pick any instrument. You've got to love it! After all, you'll be spending a lot of time with your guitar. You've got to be drawn to your instrument's sound and the way it feels in your hands. If you feel this way about the instrument you choose, you'll be more likely to stick with it.

THE PARTS OF A GUITAR

You learn about the different parts of your body in school. It's important to take good care of each of these parts. You've got to take good care of your guitar too. So you'll want to know all about its parts. Are you ready?

END PIN

The end pin is the small post where a strap can be attached to the guitar. The strap is used to help support the guitar's weight.

BRIDGE

The bridge is the metal or wooden plate that connects the strings to the guitar's body.

SOUNDING BOARD

The sounding board is on the front of the guitar's body. The sounding board helps to amplify—or increase the volume of—the guitar's sound.

STRINGS

Most guitars have six strings, though different types of guitars can have more or fewer. Guitar strings are usually made of nylon or metal wire.

HEADSTOCK and TUNING PEGS

Your head is at the top of your body. The guitar's headstock is at the top of the instrument. Tuning pegs stick out from the headstock. These help keep the guitar's strings tight. The tuning pegs are also used to tune the guitar. Guitarists turn a peg to the right or left to change the pitch of a string.

NUT

The nut is a small piece between the headstock and the neck of the guitar. The nut has grooves in it to help keep the strings in place.

FINGERBOARD

The fingerboard (also known as the fretboard) is a flat piece of wood on the guitar's neck. This is where a guitarist places his or her fingers to make notes and chords.

NECK

Your neck connects your head to your body. The guitar's neck does something like that too. It's the long barlike piece that connects the headstock to the guitar's body.

FRETS

Frets are small bars on the guitar's fingerboard. Frets show guitarists where to put their fingers to lengthen or shorten strings. This lets guitarists play different pitches (high and low notes).

CHAPTER TWO

SO MANY WAYS TO PLAY

Peanut butter and jelly. Cereal and milk. Some things just go together. The guitar and rock music are among these things. Are you learning to play the guitar? If you like rock, you've found the perfect instrument.

There are many great rock guitarists. Jimi Hendrix was among the best. Hendrix taught himself to play guitar. He experimented and came up with a style all his own. Hendrix's music excited people. He was also a super showman. Fans loved seeing him onstage. They never knew what to expect. At the 1967

Jimi Hendrix was left-handed. He chose to play a right-handed guitar upside down.

10

Monterey International Pop Music Festival in Monterey, California, Hendrix really wowed the crowd. He set his guitar on fire.

Hendrix also amazed listeners when he played other people's songs. At the 1969 Woodstock Music and Art Fair in Bethel, New York, he played "The Star-Spangled Banner." But he played it in his own way. Hendrix added howling high notes. He made his guitar sound like a zooming jet plane. When asked about the unusual performance, he simply said: "I'm an American, so I played it. . . . I thought it was beautiful." Hendrix died in 1970 of drug-related causes. He was just twenty-seven years old. Though he is no longer with us, his music lives on.

Jimi Hendrix *(left)* plays "The Star-Spangled Banner" at the 1969 Woodstock Music and Art Fair.

PLAY THE MEXICAN WAY

Do you love the guitar but want to play an instrument that's off the beaten path? If so, check out the guitarrón mexicano. It's a supersized guitar with a very deep sound.

Be warned: You need strong fingers to play this whopper of a guitar. Its strings are extra thick.

Usually the guitarrón mexicano is played in mariachi bands. These small groups of musicians play mostly Mexican folk music. But sometimes rock musicians use this guitar too. Randy Meisner of the rock band the Eagles plays the guitarrón mexicano on the track "New Kid in Town." Guitarist Roy Estrada of the rock band the Mothers of Invention has also played the instrument. It can be heard on the Mothers' 1966 album *Freak Out!*

The guitarrón mexicano adds a deep sound to Mexican mariachi music.

You've probably heard Eddie Van Halen's music. He's the lead guitarist and cofounder of the hard rock band Van Halen. Eddie Van Halen developed a dazzlingly fast guitar-playing style that made him famous. Van Halen is also famous for his terrific guitar solos. As a teen, he spent hours in his room practicing. He became one of the best rock guitarists.

Famous rock groups such as the Beatles and Led Zeppelin also made guitars a key part of their sound. Led Zeppelin's Jimmy Page helped create heavy metal music. He played bluesy rock louder and faster than most musicians before him. John Lennon and George Harrison played many types of music with the Beatles. The two guitarists' love of different styles helped make their group great.

Want to play like Van Halen, Hendrix, or other rock guitarists? Listen to their music. Try to play along with the recordings. Get a feel for what it would be like to really play rock music.

Eddie Van Halen rocks out on the guitar in 1998.

B. B. KING

Without the blues, there wouldn't be rock music. B. B. King (right) is an American blues great. He is never seen performing without his trusty guitar Lucille. King's guitar solos are unique and emotional.

King's style has inspired musicians from the Rolling Stones to John Mayer. But he is not just a guitar hero. King also works to fight the disease diabetes. He helps educate others about the illness.

COUNTRY MUSIC

These days many country artists add electric guitars and a rocking beat to their music. The result is sometimes called southern-fried country rock. But it doesn't matter what brand of country music you like. The guitar and country music go together. It's hard to think of one without the other.

Clint Black is a well-known country singer and guitarist. He's sold more than twenty million CDs worldwide. Black is a country music performer who rocks. But at times, he also plays more traditional country sounds.

Taylor Swift is another singer with a passion for guitar. Pop fans and country fans both enjoy her upbeat songs. Does that sound like the best of both worlds? If so, try playing some country music yourself. See what works best for you. You may come up with your own style.

Clint Black jams on an electric guitar at a country music festival in 2005.

Taylor Swift performs at the 2010 Grammy Awards. Her album Fearless won Album of the Year.

MEET THE BANJO

Are you a fool for toe-tapping, knee-slapping bluegrass music? Want to play an instrument that's perfect for this bright, twangy sound? Then think about taking up the banjo.

There are many different types of banjos to choose from. Among these are four- and five-string banjos. There's even a six-string banjo that's played like a guitar.

JAZZ GUITAR

Quick! Think of a jazz instrument. Did a saxophone or trumpet come to mind? Hey, wait a minute—this book is about the guitar! Is there room for a guitarist in the jazz scene? You bet there is. Guitarists have played in jazz ensembles and as soloists.

Django Reinhardt was a guitarist from Europe who fell in love with American jazz. In 1928 a fire burned Reinhardt's left hand. He could not use two of his fingers. But instead of giving up the guitar, Reinhardt created a new, one-of-a-kind playing style. After recovering, Reinhardt played across Europe with an all-string jazz band.

Jazz guitarists have many chances to express themselves when they perform. At times, these guitarists make up their music as they play. This is known as improvisation. Improvisation gives jazz guitarists a chance to really own the music.

Could jazz be your thing? If so, spend some time listening to jazz guitar music. See which guitarists you like best. Can you copy their style? After a while, try improvising too.

This all-female jazz band features a guitar *(left)*. It also includes drums, a double bass, and a saxophone.

CLASSICAL GUITAR

Have you always liked classical music? You may be a classy kid who ends up playing classical guitar. The early classical composers did not write much music for the guitar. That was partly because guitars weren't used in orchestras. The guitar was largely seen as a folk instrument.

But things changed with time. Some guitarists adapted classical pieces for the guitar. Spanish musician Andrés Segovia became legendary for his classical guitar playing. During his career, Segovia performed the music of famous composers such as Johann Sebastian Bach, Wolfgang Amadeus Mozart, and Frédéric Chopin. Composers began writing new music for the guitar in the classical style as well. These days, a classical guitarist has lots of music to choose from.

Classical guitarist Sharon Isbin performs at the 2010 Grammy Awards in Los Angeles, California.

Do you hope to become a great classical guitarist? If so, listen to different classical guitarists. Try playing along with them. You'll have fun and learn a lot too.

A TIMELESS INSTRUMENT

The guitar is not a new instrument. People have played string instruments for hundreds of years. A guitarlike instrument called the *vihuela* was popular in Spain in the 1400s. The vihuela had twelve strings. By the 1500s, the guitar was taking shape across Europe. Over the years, it came to look a lot like modern acoustic (nonelectric) guitars.

Guitar music changed a lot in the 1930s. That's when electric guitars arrived on the scene. These guitars have special devices called pickups. Pickups send the sounds guitar strings make as electrical signals to electric amplifiers.

The electric guitar could be played along with much louder instruments. It began to be regularly used in country, jazz, blues, and rock bands. Wherever you hear popular music these days, listen for the guitar. You're likely to hear it!

Pickups give the electric guitar its loud sound.

CHAPTER THREE

YOU AND THE GUITAR

The guitar is really popular among young people. Chances are some of your friends or family members play it already. People choose their instruments for lots of different reasons. Let's take a closer look at why so many people pick the guitar.

MUSIC EARLY ON

Some kids come from homes where just about everyone plays an instrument. That's how it was for guitarist Joe

This man is showing his son how to play guitar. Many children start playing an instrument because other people in the family play it.

20

Tunon. "I was born into a musical household," he said. "Both my parents played piano. As soon as I could reach the keys, I started banging away on the piano. For a long time, it was a fun toy for me. Then at sixteen, I got my first guitar. I really enjoyed playing it. The six strings on my guitar were even more fun than the eighty-eight piano keys had been."

Guitarist Jesse Hale also had a musical background. "My grandfather played piano when nobody was around," he remarked. "I would listen to him play music late at night. Everyone else in the house had gone to bed. I loved hearing him and knew that I wanted music in my life. But for me, it would be the guitar."

Many people fall in love with playing the guitar.

DON'T JUST HEAR—LISTEN!

Good guitarists are also good listeners. Just take it from the pros:

"Music is in everything around us. Musicians have to have a good ear. They've got to be tuned into all kinds of sounds. The wind has a sound. Even silence has a sound. Train yourself to hear these sounds."
—Cesar Rios, guitarist

"Good musicians spend a lot of time listening to others play. This can be very useful. It can help you come up with new ideas for your own music."
—Tom Mazzeo, guitarist

MUSIC UP CLOSE

Lots of other things have turned kids on to music and the guitar. Sometimes, it's seeing a live performance. That's what did it for guitarist Alex Kash. "I was just six years old when it happened for me," he said. "A few local musicians came to my school. They played some classical music. They also did some patriotic tunes. Those musicians were wonderful. I was so excited after hearing them. From that day on, I told everyone that I was going to be a musician."

COST COUNTS

For many kids, the cost of an instrument matters. Maybe they can't afford their first choice. But they can always get a decent guitar for a good price.

Price was a problem for guitarist Cesar Rios. "At first, I wanted to play the piano," Rios recalled. "But I didn't have a piano. I couldn't afford to buy one either. I was able to buy a guitar, though."

This girl is trying out a guitar at a guitar store.

The guitar proved to be a great choice for Rios. Playing it became an important outlet for him. "When I was stressed out, I'd just grab my guitar," he said. "It was a terrific escape. It took me away from everything. It still does."

IT'S GOTTA BE RIGHT FOR YOU

No matter what instrument you choose, it has to feel right to you. Guitarist Neil Kaplan described what playing the guitar means to him. "All musical instruments are special," Kaplan noted. "But for me, playing the guitar has been great.

A HELPFUL HINT: PLAY THE CLASSICAL WAY

Are you a jazz nut? Or a rock-and-roll kid who only wants to play the rock way? You may be surprised by what you can learn from playing classical music. "Get your training in classical guitar," suggested classical guitarist Carlos Molina. "It doesn't matter if you want to play rock or jazz. Being properly trained can only help you. Some college music programs require students to take two years of classical training. They must complete this before they can begin to study jazz."

LATIN FOLK MUSIC

Do you love folk music? Does the music of the Andes Mountains move you? If so, you might want to try a smaller relative of the guitar known as the *charango* (*right*). This instrument is widely used to play folk music in the mountains of Peru and Bolivia.

It lets me express my feelings. Through the guitar, my fingers show what's in my heart. My emotions become the sound of my instrument. I can share my feelings with others without saying a word."

Is that how you feel about your guitar? Do you love the time you spend playing it? Do you want to be able to play it really well? If so, you've picked the right instrument.

CHAPTER FOUR

BEING A GUITARIST

Time for a quick quiz: What instrument do most kids say they wish they could play?

  A. guitar

  B. flute

  C. piano

  D. violin

  E. oboe

If your answer was the guitar, you're right! But as you know, wishing doesn't make it so. If you want to play the guitar well, effort is required.

Music stores offer all kinds of guitars to choose from.

26

PRACTICE MAKES PERFECT

Practice is essential to anyone who wants to play the guitar. If you don't practice, you won't get very far. Different people need different amounts of practice time. Some players quickly learn how to position their fingers and play the right notes. They might not need to spend as much time learning basic skills. Others may take longer to learn proper guitar technique. They might need to practice more at first—but in time, they can wind up being the best players.

For most new students, about a half an hour to forty-five minutes of practice a day will usually do. All new guitar students should practice their scales (groups of notes that go up or down in order). It's also important to go over any material you don't know well yet.

Practice is important for any guitar player.

Try to practice every day. That's better than practicing four hours on the day before your lesson. Through practice, you train both your mind and hands to play guitar. In time, you'll be able to do things on your guitar without even thinking about it. And before you know it, practicing might become a highlight of your day, "After a terrible day, I'll just sit down and play," said guitarist Matt Johnson. "It brings me a wonderful sense of peace."

The more often you practice, the more fun you might have.

POLISH YOUR PEOPLE SKILLS

You need more than musical skills to succeed in music. People skills are almost as important. Most of the time, you'll be playing with other musicians. Here are some tips to follow when playing in a band:

- Remember to be on time for your practice sessions. It's annoying to have to waste time waiting for someone.
- Be sure you know your part well. That means practicing on your own beforehand.
- Listen to what the other musicians have to say. Their opinions and feelings count too.
- Most important, don't demand star treatment for yourself. That kind of behavior never gets anyone very far in a band. It's even been known to get some people bounced out of bands.

IF IT CAN HAPPEN, IT WILL HAPPEN

Let's say you've practiced for months. You know your material inside out. You feel ready to perform for an audience. Being so well prepared, you're sure that nothing will go wrong. This performance and all your future performances will always be perfect. Right?

Don't count on it. No matter how well prepared you are, things can and will go wrong. Guitar strings have broken during shows. Musicians have tripped over cords. Some have even fallen off the stage.

Outdoor performances are well known for their problems. At times, the wind has blown away sheet music. Music stands have fallen over. Bands have been soaked during sudden thunderstorms. Equipment has been damaged or destroyed in bad weather as well.

It's always a good idea to try to expect the unexpected. Guitarist Johnny Gale saw something he never expected when he was just starting out. "I was in a band when I was thirteen and naturally wasn't a very experienced performer," Gale recalled. "None of the guys in our band were. One of them sang and played the electric guitar.

KEEP LEARNING

Guitarist Alex Kash believes that even the most experienced guitarists always have more to learn. "Music is a lifetime learning experience," he explained. "I learn every time I play. The more you learn, the easier it is to create something beautiful."

The Rolling Stones perform in a rainstorm in 1995.

If you do this, you have to make sure your equipment is grounded (properly plugged into an outlet to help prevent electrical shock). But he didn't check before we started playing. He began singing with his microphone on. If he hadn't been wearing braces, it would have been bad enough. But when his braces touched the microphone, we all saw a spark shoot out of his mouth. Ouch! I think that taught him a lesson. I know that I learned something that day. Respect electricity."

Musicians aren't strangers to mishaps. They can happen to anyone at any time. "Once when I was performing, I lost sight of where the edge of the stage was," remembered guitarist Matthew Sabatella. "One of my legs went over the edge. Luckily, I bounced from the floor back onto the stage.

But I didn't fully regain my balance. I hopped on one leg for a few steps before falling down behind the drum set. I kept playing my guitar through the whole thing, though. The show must go on."

Some things are out of your control. When they happen, there isn't much you can do. But you can try to prepare for other things. "One of the most likely things to go wrong at a performance is breaking a guitar string," according to Sabatella. "If a string breaks during a performance, the guitar is harder to play. It goes out of tune more easily. I try to avoid breaking strings during a performance. I always put brand-new strings on my guitar before going onstage. Older strings are more likely to break."

Other times, you can become distracted during a performance and lose focus. As Johnny Gale explained, "You can have fun while playing, but don't fool around. Try to stay focused on what you're doing. It's very important to remain aware of what's going on around you. If you are nervous, get into the music and let it take you to a happy place. Try to relax, yet concentrate. This is a vital combination for a great performance. You can do it if you try."

Performances can be lots of fun when you are ready to handle the unexpected.

WORDS OF WISDOM

Guitarist Dennis Weislik has this advice for young guitarists who dream of performing onstage: "Try to be as well-rounded as possible. Learn to play jazz and country music [in addition to rock and heavy metal]. You never know what a job will call for. If you're well-prepared, you'll have a better chance at success."

Don't let mishaps ruin your performance. Try to take whatever happens in stride. If you make a mistake, keep on playing. Often the audience won't even realize it. Those people came to hear good music. Always do your best to deliver that.

BE TRUE TO YOURSELF

Your success in music is really up to you. You'll get out of the guitar what you put into it. Never forget that your music can be a wonderful gift for both you and those who hear you. As Tom Mazzeo put it, "Great music is more than just notes and rhythms. It's an expression of what's inside the musician. The best musicians let their inner spirit come through the music they perform. They trust what they have inside."

Trust yourself, work hard, and enjoy what you're doing. That's a great recipe for success.

QUIZ: IS THE GUITAR RIGHT FOR YOU?

Which of these statements describes you best? Please record your answers on a separate sheet of paper.

1. If at first you don't succeed,
- **A.** You try, try again. You like to finish what you start. People say you're the determined type.
- **B.** You feel that a lack of success means it wasn't meant to be. You prefer to try something else you may be better at.

2. When you hear a good piece of music,
- **A.** You get really into all the sounds. You feel as if you could listen to the piece forever!
- **B.** You think it sounds good, but you don't usually get too absorbed in it. You'd rather spend time working on art or learning new soccer moves than listening closely to music.

3. When you're doing a task that requires fine motor skills,
- **A.** Your fingers are quick and nimble. Detailed tasks are fun for you.
- **B.** You tend to drop things or get frustrated. Taking bike rides or playing soccer is more up your alley than working with your hands.

4. When you're working toward a long-term goal,
- **A.** You tend to be patient. It doesn't bother you to practice a skill again and again.
- **B.** You get a little antsy. You'd rather move on to something new than focus on the same task for a long time.

5. When you think about practicing your instrument,
- **A.** You get really excited. You think studying an instrument sounds like fun!
- **B.** You like music, but you can think of other things you'd rather do. Giving up free time to practice every day doesn't sound worth it.

Were your answers mostly A's?

If so, the guitar may just be the right choice for you!

GLOSSARY

amplify: to increase the volume of a sound

bluegrass: a form of U.S. country music

blues: a form of music created by African Americans often performed on guitar

bridge: the metal or wooden plate that connects the strings to the guitar's body

classical: a form of European music often performed by an orchestra or throughout an opera

end pin: the post where a strap can be attached to the guitar

fingerboard: the flat piece of wood on a guitar's neck where a guitarist places his or her fingers to play notes. The fingerboard is also known as the fretboard.

frets: small bars on the guitar's fingerboard that show guitarists where to put their fingers to play different pitches

headstock: the part of a guitar above the fingerboard where strings attach to tuning pegs

improvisation: making up parts of the music you play while you are playing it

jazz: a form of music characterized by loose structure and improvisation

pickup: a device on an electric guitar's body that sends the sound a string makes to an amplifier

pitch: the highness or lowness of a sound

scale: a group of musical notes going up or down in order

solo: a musical performance in which a performer plays alone

string family: a group of instruments that produce sound through the movement of their strings

tuning peg: a peg on the guitar that is used to tune a string

SOURCE NOTES

11 Jimi Hendrix, television interview with Dick Cavett, *The Dick Cavett Show*, September 9, 1969, http://www.youtube.com/watch?v=B-ZYUaRKQkk (January 14, 2010).

21 Joe Tunon, e-mail message to author, August 12, 2009.

21 Jesse Hale, interview with author, June 11, 2009.

22 Cesar Rios, interview with author, July 4, 2009.

22 Tom Mazzeo, e-mail message to author, September 27, 2009.

23 Alex Kash, e-mail message to author, July 17, 2009.

23–24 Rios.

24 Ibid.

24 Carlos Molina, interview with author, June 16, 2009.

24–25 Neil Kaplan, e-mail message to author, July 29, 2009.

28 Matt Johnson, interview with author, June 2, 2009.

30 Kash.

30–31 Johnny Gale, e-mail message to author, September 11, 2009.

31–32 Matthew Sabatella, e-mail message to author, May 27, 2009.

32 Ibid.

32 Gale.

33 Dennis Weislik, interview with author, June 4, 2009.

33 Mazzeo.

SELECTED BIBLIOGRAPHY

Bacon, Tony. *2,000 Guitars*. San Diego: Thunder Bay Press, 2009.

Fisher, Jody. *Beginning Jazz Guitar*. Van Nuys, CA: Alfred Publishing Company, 2006.

Kolb, Tom. *Music Theory for Guitarists: Everything You Wanted to Know but Were Afraid to Ask*. Milwaukee: Hal Leonard Corporation, 2005.

Sandberg, Larry. *The Acoustic Guitar Guide: Everything You Need to Know to Buy and Maintain a New or Used Guitar*. Chicago: Chicago Review Press, 2000.

Schiller, David. *Guitars: A Celebration of Pure Mojo*. New York: Workman Publishing Company, 2008.

Stetina, Troy. *Total Rock Guitar: A Complete Guide to Learning Rock Guitar*. Milwaukee: Hal Leonard Corporation, 2001.

FOR MORE INFORMATION:

Christensen, Bonnie. *Django: World's Greatest Jazz Guitarist*. New York: Roaring Brook, 2009. This book gives readers an interesting and refreshing look at the life of the outstanding jazz guitarist Django Reinhardt. Special attention is paid to his unique jazz sound and technique.

Enchanted Learning: Make a Box Guitar
http://www.enchantedlearning.com/crafts/Boxguitar.shtml
Learn how a guitar works by making your own box guitar. All you'll need is a few household items.

George-Warren, Holly. *Honky-tonk Heroes and Hillbilly Angels: The Pioneers of Country and Western Music*. Boston: Houghton Mifflin, 2006. This book provides short but interesting biographies of important figures in country-and-western music. There's also information on the roots and development of this music.

Kenney, Karen Latchana. *Cool Rock Music: Create and Appreciate What Makes Music Great!* Edina, MN: Abdo, 2008. This book introduces rock music and the instruments used to play it. There's also info on writing a rock song and making a rock video.

Landau, Elaine. *Is the Violin for You?* Minneapolis: Lerner Publications Company, 2011. If the guitar isn't right for you, check out another string instrument: violin. This book from the Ready to Make Music series covers violin basics, including what the instrument looks like and what music it is used to play.

THE GUITARISTS WHO HELPED WITH THIS BOOK

This book could not have been written without the help of these talented guitarists.

FEDERICO BONACOSSA
Classical guitarist Federico Bonacossa has performed in numerous venues. He is also pursuing his doctoral degree in classical guitar.

DAVEE BRYAN
Guitarist Davee Bryan has created and played original music for more than thirty years. He has toured in the United States, Europe, and the Middle East.

JOHNNY GALE
Guitarist, songwriter, and musical director Johnny Gale has been a force in rock music since the 1960s. He's also a noted expert in the R&B field.

JESSE HALE
Jesse Hale is a guitarist and music educator. He is pursuing his doctorate in guitar performance.

NEIL KAPLAN
Guitarist Neil Kaplan is the founder and music director of New Attitude Productions. The company provides live music and entertainment for events throughout South Florida.

ALEX KASH
Alex Kash is a guitarist and songwriter. He writes and performs in a variety of styles and genres.

TOM MAZZEO
Tom Mazzeo plays rhythm guitar with the rock band the 540s. He is also a music educator.

CARLOS MOLINA
Carlos Molina is on the music faculty of Miami-Dade Community College. He is also the founder of the Miami Classical Guitar Society.

CESAR RIOS
Guitarist Cesar Rios plays in a variety of styles including salsa, flamenco, disco, and rock. In addition to performing in the United States, he's also appeared in New Zealand, Australia, Canada, Mexico, and other countries.

MATTHEW SABATELLA
Matthew Sabatella is an award-winning singer and guitarist. He's the creator of BalladofAmerica.com, through which he uses folk music to inspire people about the past.

JOE TUNON
Joe Tunon is a guitarist and songwriter. He is known as Jukebox Joe for the variety of rock songs he performs.

DENNIS WEISLIK
Dennis Weislik is a guitarist and songwriter who plays rock, jazz, blues, and country music. He has performed in the bands of numerous well-known artists.

INDEX

PHOTO ACKNOWLEDGMENTS

The images in this book are used with the permission of: © iStockphoto.com/pixhook, p. 1; © Koufax73/Dreamstime.com, p. 3; © Jose Manuel Gelpi Diaz/Dreamstime.com, p. 4; © ABBAS MOMANI/AFP/Getty Images, p. 5; © Laura Frenkel/Dreamstime.com, p. 6; AP Photo/Keystone, Laurent Gillieron, p. 7; © Mikhail Dudarev/Dreamstime.com, pp. 8–9; MARC SHARRATT/Rex Features USA, p. 10; © Barry Z Levine/Premium Archive/Getty Images, p. 11; AP Photo/Jeff Geisler, p. 12; Rex Features USA, pp. 13, 15 (right); © Barry Brecheisen/ WireImage/Getty Images, p. 14; AP Photo/Matt Sayles, p. 15 (left); © Wolfgang Amri/ Dreamstime.com, p. 16; © PM Images/Stone/Getty Images, p. 17; © Kevin Winter/Getty Images, p. 18; © Jonathan White/Dreamstime.com, p. 19; © Alistair Berg/Digital Vision/Getty Images, p. 20; © Rayes/Photodisc/Getty Images, p. 21; © Inti St. Clair/Digital Vision/Getty Images, p. 22; © Jupiter Images/Brand X Pictures/Getty Images, pp. 23, 26; © Kwheatley/ Dreamstime.com, p. 25 (top); © Jenny Acheson/Riser/Getty Images, p. 25 (bottom); © GAETAN BALLY/Keystone/CORBIS, p. 27; © Rennie Solis/Photodisc/Getty Images, p. 28; © Oleg Shelomentsev/Dreamstime.com, p. 30; © FORESTIER YVES/CORBIS SYGMA, p. 31; © Marissa Kaiser/Stone/Getty Images, p. 32.

Front cover: © iStockphoto.com/pixhook.